RAMBLING JOT THOUGHTS

OF LOVE

WITH NO ENDING

BY
DR. ROGER S. PRITCHARD

authorHOUSE®

AuthorHouse™
1663 Liberty Drive
Bloomington, IN 47403
www.authorhouse.com
Phone: 1-800-839-8640

First published by AuthorHouse   04/27/2011

ISBN: 978-1-4567-5271-2 (sc)

Printed in the United States of America

I'LL FORGET
Love You, I did
Love Me, I think you did.
But funny now
How a plain and simple love,
With Neither to blame,
Could become so twisted.

I'll forget
About the
First Time.
But
On the second time,
If it doesn't work out Forever,
I'll forget it.

LOOKS
Caught looks of you – Last nite,
Couldn't help but notice
Your looks could last past the nite.

Thanks for the Looks - You gave
I couldn't help but notice.

BELONGS
You may always have ME
To always be in love with Me
You may not.
Where you are – You may meet another
Then where will your heart belong?
To ME?
It belongs
If you'll only give it this time.

GOOD LOOKING
You have
Good Looks
Keep Looking

TOMORROW MAYBE
I can hardly wait
Till you knock on my door
If it be tomorrow
Or
I only wish it were the Day Before.

DARE
Now that I see Love
I dare to look.
It's . . . . I dread
The Long Journey

The Train of love
Moves slow.
There's too many
Whistle Stops.

SWEET THOUGHTS
Sweet thoughts
Of
Memories
Is
Love
So I Jot
These thoughts.

THIS TIME

I thought I'd lost
I never thought you cared this June.
Belief in what you've said —
That is, if it's me you really want.
This time, I'll give you all of me
And wish us Love — FOREVER.

IF I SHOULD KNOCK

My Love, We assume
That tomorrow--We'll Meet Again.

But if, per chance,
You should knock and I'm gone,
I'd like to take today to say
I LOVE YOU

CLOSE

That year I remember
The rains were late. It rained most of May.
I know how close the Rains brought us,
We'd lay in close the whole day.

As the rains danced down our windows,
We vowed we'd never be apart.
It's raining now — You are not here.
Yes you are! But — it's only in my heart.

CLOSE BY MILES

To of been so long together,
Yet so far apart.
Then, to be so far apart.
Those miles seem to bring us closer.
BUT
The space between—Doesn't kiss you goodnight
NOR
Lay beside you—thru a cold winter's nite.

OLE LETTERS

Some old letters I wrote so long ago
The words seem to say the same
Funny how—now, the feelings change
Not the words.

ALL NIGHT

I never knew how good
To have you alone thru the night
Till I became
—ALONE—
Through the night.

WORDS ON WINGS

Across the miles—I hope my letters race
To bring you words—each and every day.
With the stroke from my pen,
The words will last thru the years.

LOOKING

As I wait here for you,
There's nothing that can stop my memories.
As I wait thru the nite, there's nothing that can stop
My dreams of you.
Even if years go by, there's nothing that can catch
My eye.
There's nothing at all that can stop
My looking for you.

LASTING KISS

If, you'll pull your shades,
I'll kiss you good night.
A kiss from the past
That's travelled down thru the years.

MILES APART

You are gone.
Have a lovely time
All the way,

Sunny skies every day,
New sights to see,
New things to learn.

One is, I LOVE YOU!
And then a happy and safe return
To ME –
You are needed on your returning.

OLE TRACES

The rusty ole tracks still run there.
The train is gone now,
The cold stone station is dark and empty.

As I wait by the tracks
You don't come running.
Then, in the breaking dawn, the train roars in.

You stepping down–smiling-glowing-projecting
Your love.
Then I open my eyes and SEE,
It's only in my heart.

PREFACE

I've just begun.
Maybe there is little to say –
More than in my thoughts
Jotted down as the words came,
Unarranged

It's best to say, it's like a jigsaw puzzle
With pieces missing and pieces that don't fit.

GRAND STREET

Grand Street is still there –The bar is gone.
It's a lonesome Place
-The Street-

It's called by another name now.
You and I met there.
Now as I walk alone–thru the nite
Your footsteps, don't follow.

Where once–we seemed to have Happiness,
There are shadows and stillness.

And as I stop, look into the darkness,
Listening long into the night with the dawn,
I find it's all gone, except in my heart.

ONE WAY FARE

It was late fall, Halloween just passed.
That night, first frost.

You're in town—on a round trip.
You stay at the bar, return ticket in hand.

No one was out, we talked,
I guess the night was right.

We tore the ticket apart, returned,
One-way fare.

Yes, all that night, til frosty morning
And since—

Not one separate moment
Have we been since apart
Thank you heart.

I miss you so—
You're not here;
The frost is.

RICHES

Rich in life—Rich in Love
Yet Poor in Acceptance.

There comes a time you know
When they offer no more.

ECHOES

Long now since you're gone.
I hear the sounds through the night.
Your voice rings,

Like bells on night air.
Funny, I wonder? If each had seconds
Would the minutes pass, like the first?

BELONGED

We lived upstairs; there I felt I belonged.
You wanted me there.
Me failing to notice; You felt unnoticed.
If I'd only known.

So now, only in my heart you belong.
I let you go away—unnoticed.

Me failing to realize you were gone
Till I was not wanted.
Then too late, I felt, If only I
Belonged.

FOR AWHILE

I'm sort of tired;
I never was very good.
Guess I'll Rest
For awhile.

WAITING

A candle for you burns in my window
From the hard dark road outside.

It lites the way thru the night
Should you be passing by.
Look close—You'll see my face
In the candle glow.

HOT AUGUST

August here, like the ones past.
We kissed the first one,
Hot August, with hot kisses.

Augusts, with you, there were many.
Some I can't focus.

This August, I'll remember
You went away. I guess—

My kisses grew cold.
I wish we'd grown

OLDER
NOT
COLDER

FIRST WORDS

Today, word from you.
With lonesome hands and lonely fingers,
I tore the wrapper away.

Saw with clouds across my eyes,
You saying, "I was your sunshine."
Across the front a sill-o-ette
With words, "You are on my mind."
In your hand, words saying,
Belief of what you said,
"Take me as needed."
My eyes cry and dry,
BUT–MY-HEART-WON'T-STOP

SILL-O-ETTE

I see you standing still,
A sill-o-ette
Against the English skies,
Watching the ducks and ducklings
Swimming there near the Rye.

How fast the young learn.
Few mistakes, they have
To learn from.

PROTECTION

Hello's encounter a way toward many goodbyes.
Like needs, leading to wants.
How much safer to want.
People don't expect as much from you then.

A RAINY DAY

A rainy day, for us, I've placed away
To keep for us always.

Not of the summer,
But from the Spring of mind
Cause there I can remember.

If it should be me, you wish,
I'll give all myself and keep the rainy day
FOREVER.

GOING

A day not long ago
You told me you were going.
Your eyes begged to stay.

Inside I cried, was afraid if
I asked you not,
That you couldn't say no.

Then again, you'd yearn.
I was afraid to cry again.

So stood and bade a false
FAREWELL.
Now I cry for you.

STRAWBERRY TIME

Your strawberry smile
Always gave you away each year.
You had a surprise of strawberry time.
It was your first love, other than I.

I've never been to Ole London town
I wonder?
Do they have strawberries there?

Do you sit at Piccadilly Square
As Big Ben strikes?
Is it strawberry time?

Your fresh strawberry smile
Stays in my mind.
I'm still here, for you see,
IT'S STRAWBERRY TIME

GIVING THANKS

Thank you there—for, today, words came
From the one I love.

It seals a smile inside.
I know the tones and tints of that smile
Must show—Even if it should fade.

SONGS

Many songs have I to sing,
Many smiles have I to smile,
Not many loves have I,
ONLY
YOU

I.O.U.

If you don't want me.
Let me know
This you owe.

IF UNS

If uns you're short
If not—I'd like something
From a land I've never been.

Don't say it, bring it Home with you.
I wait, caught short of you.
Please come home to me soon.

SHADOW

As I browse and from the window shop,
I catch a glimpse of your ever present shadow.

I find the objects bought turn out to be
The things I thought you mite have liked.

LEAVES

Our life together was like a tree budding in Spring.
Then in the Summer of our romance, the
Leaves stirred gently.

They all seemed to fit,
Closing Summer, brought fading colors.
Then they began to fall.
Now in the Winter of our life, many years later,
I wish I'd caught each leaf
And placed them away
FOREVER . . .

BATTLES

Wars go on inside me,
Some I win, some I lose.

Yet, they go on; no matter how
Hard I try to stop them.

There is one war I shouldn't
Be afraid to lose . . . .
The war of loving you.

MELODY

It's my sounds
My memories
My music
My songs,

That I hear long after the noise is gone.
They belong to me, and another person.

That I spent more than fifteen years
Of mine and their life together.
Whether it be friend, lover, or a person.

Each of us has the past pleasures that
Seem to go away and yet, recall.

The sounds of childhood,
Love or friend,
Can be music to our ears.
This is in hope.

In all its roughness
That the melody
Will play on.
I HAVE YOU ALL THE WAY.

LOST REWARD

From the meeting of you brought hope
Life can be good I say.
I can't say . . .
But one thing I can say,
The need of knowing anyone, but you,
Is what I've lost.

I'M LONESOME

I walked along the river today;
The trees are supplying it a winter coat.
I'm Lonesome
Running its regular life's course,
Staying within its banks,
No rush, moving steadily along.
I'm Lonesome
The fish stir busily, sometimes in schools,
sometimes alone.
Yet, the water runs on, unnoticing its friends.
I'm Lonesome
Swimming on its top, the ducks are
Making their last search for food.
Changing not its steady movement, only its surface.
I'm Lonesome
What a large bend ahead, will it make it?
Bending as needed, it continues on, undisturbed.
I'm Lonesome
What a smooth life,
So at peace, so regular, so in balance.
I'm Lonesome
Could I have been wrong? A fork is approaching,
I'm Lonesome
It's separating, some one way, some the other.
No crisis, no explosion, no high nor lows.
It's smiling and saying, "Thanks for staying with me
As long as you were able."
"We'll meet again someday, if destiny wills it.
I'm Lonesome?
NOT ANY MORE
Destiny call me.

31

SAD EYES

I've been looking for my pride.
If I can find it,
I'll see what value is left
For me.
A childhood, yes, I have missed that.
Maybe . . . .
That is why
I could not grow up!

Who knows ALL the answers
Of these questions I have to ask?
Do you?

Will I accept them . . .
If you do, answer them?
Do you really see
Things as they really are?
Or
Are you protecting me?
From hurt and pain, sadness, and loneliness?

A filtering system for the heart,
From the past, in the present,
Or
Of the future?
To function outward and never inward, is
Blindness with sight,
Sad Eyes . . . . .

I RECKON

I read again the words, written in black,
On red paper, background of white,
In a brown frame hanging on the lonely wall.

The "Rambling Thoughts" supply the proper setting,
From August to September 21ˢᵗ the postmarks reveal.
Constant communication, just a passing parting,
No ending, time to prepare for a new beginning.

The mailman smiles as he passes me by as if to say
"Maybe Tomorrow"
Tomorrow, I'm waiting as usual to wait another day.
I don't mind, I've spent half my life fighting
And half waiting.
The fighting has left me, but the waiting remains.

I'm becoming quite a good friend to myself,
Working together instead of apart.
Who knows, I may even begin to like that other me?
He's not all that bad, you know.

A little obstinate at times, pre-judging,
Without all the facts.
Sometimes he's right; sometimes he's wrong;
Regardless, the simple fact that he cares, is sufficient.

I look into the mirror and wonder, "Why can't others,
See what story is being told, through these eyes?"
Then a tear falls from them; I Cry Out, for
What I'm trying to project and relay, and then receive.

Maybe one goes thru life associating
What they have missed for
What they think they want?
I've missed nothing in life; it has all come my way at
One time or another.
Just unable to comprehend and keep what I wanted.

REFLECTIONS

Up this morning, hoping the loneliness will have lessened.
The sun is out—the wind is high—
The leaves, going in many directions.

I ask myself, looking out of the window,
"Is that the way of Life?"
A cup of coffee—a cigarette—reach for the pen and paper.

Oh, how I wish to put down my thoughts and
Solve the inner problems
That so inhabit my mind, as one can with Math.
No, it won't add up, no matter how I figure it.

Somewhere there is a factor or a mistake,
So the answer will never be right till I re-do it correctly.
"Time, please allow me enough time, to accomplish this."
Combination of great minds create great things.

Great Love we had, but never combined the minds to climb
Mountains, swim rivers, or even walk peacefully,
Hand in hand.
How lucky the small parts that entered my life, good
Or bad, who's to say, even if not to linger forever?

You can remove the physical, but the mental you can
Never have back.
It is a part that belongs to me, which I shall hold onto
The rest of my life. I never meant to hurt—just love.

Looking into the mirror—it's difficult to answer
All the questions that reflection looking at me is asking.
Someday, someway, somehow,
Maybe it will be able to smile and say,
"Thanks for solving all the
Questions, discontent, and loneliness,
Keep it this way.

FRIDAY

I drove two miles today, down along the river,
Over the bridge, under the railroad tracks
To the round-a-bout.
I stayed to the left and turned at the light.
Next to the park, I waited an hour or so.
Many went in and out; I just waited.

Hoping to see you, yet knowing you weren't coming.
I'm glad you didn't and I did not go in.
Neither of us belong there, especially you.
Another day perhaps? But for now,
The security of my flat waits in the darkness
Alone and empty.

I woke this morning, wanting you
as I often do from morning to night.
I wish that Friday night before you left,
I had re-arranged myself to have been closer to you
As I had met at the park gathering.

Re-arranged to whatever you must have wanted.
Or
Must have expected-but the encounter filled my head.

You told me the score, yet your call gave me hope.
Selfish isn't it? . . . That first meeting
I've remained open, waiting, for a chance to move in
close
I cannot walk another tight rope, gently give in quietly
or go.

ALONE AGAIN
Four walls, a radio, and a teli,
Yet alone again
A bite to eat, a cup of coffee
Yet alone again
Cigarette? Maybe two and a game of solitaire
Yet alone again
The phone rings, wow! Wrong number
Yet, alone again
A bath, shave, who knows may show
Yet, alone again
Wind the clock, read awhile, try to sleep
Yet, alone again
Oh well, tomorrow's near, I can begin
Yet alone again

THIS MIND
Funny what such a grey blob can do?
Never seems to rest, just works on.
Gathering information, some never to be used again.
Other, to be used when needed with reserve.

How does one pick from it for survival? Yet, not even a
vine can
Survive when stripped totally.

I feed it often to replace what I use, but I think it
often needs a diet.
It surely cannot manage more un-happiness.
What else had been available, from me?
I'll try! New sources, new happenings,
Hang on, for you're the only one I have.

????A DREAM????

I drove to the lake today,
Have not been there since the drive we took.
Nothing has changed;
the water is beautiful, the grass, leaves have. Oh Yes!
There was not the rain; lots of clouds, but not rain.

I woke this A M to a dream. In present, I followed
all that seemed real.
But after a time, I knew it was a dream.
No Grand Prix from L A, nor a beautiful cajoy in
jean, just an empty place that was not to become real.
The last encounter at this location was to
become life for me. For a short time.

I have always heard of hallucinations, and stories,
that obsess the mind.
Now I understand them as my thoughts are
Pre-occupied with this.
Obsession that it was not Real.
Just a game that was played.

Maybe time will prove it did not happen?
Collecting tidbits to sustain the myth.
Reaching out, rolling over, calling out, checking the
mail box, listening for the telephone, searching in a
crowd, driving in traffic, answering the door. You are
not there.

I'll go there again, probably many more times.
I would hate to discover you are real and I would not
Have been there to at least had a glance of you.
Are you really real????

'I SUPPOSE SO'

Love they say is a "State of Mind?"
Love, in the mind, directed in many directions, I
suppose.
Hate, is it anything opposite love? Hum! I wonder?
Can one both love and hate at the same time?
I suppose so.

In life's path, many people, things, happenings occur
that we love.
They come and they go. Yet, we allow some to linger
longer than others.
Some, we send quickly away . . . I suppose so.

Hate, here you are again; you know I don't like, want,
nor need you!
Why do you return and refuse to go? You can't stay!
Visit?
I suppose so.

LEARN TO LIVE
IN THE HERE AND NOW

Most are invariably not of the now, but of the
"what would happen if."
Learning to live in the
"Now, rather than Suppose"
Can end this.
By spending too much time in
Past and making visits to the future of the
Valuable present is
Lost.

SOMEONE-SOMEWHERE

I know there's a late blooming flower
Somewhere who needs me.
If you are it, you must not wait to tell me
For there's so little time left in this life.

Good-bye or hello . . .
How else can I say it?
To give reasons would only
Complicate my life, your life and his.

I shall not go along the river again,
which leads to the road, to the park.
For I believe in miracles
And they don't happen again, at the same place.

Again next year, the same month,
The same day, the same time,
Two other lovers will meet
At the same place.

I wonder, will they choose
A Friday night at 10:30?
If so, I hope they remember
Friday always comes, once a week

. . . and that you can count on.

SOCIALLY

Must I behave as all men do?
O K, I'll socially do as expected.
Except . . . .
Until someone passes, I can help.

D R E A M

I had a dream
And
It was of you.

It seemed to begin
Over and over
Not going very far each time.

But I tried and tried
To complete it.
Awake, I realize why it could not be total.
It was, I, dreaming it alone.

HANDS

Two appendages of this lonely body;
Ten digits you contain.
You have a gentle touch, sometimes a starving clinch!

You're quite compatible, you know?
One knows at all times what the other is doing.

Quite fortunate to work so well together
No mountains too tall for the both of you.
How lucky in sickness or injury
To be able to rely so on the other.

So many performances you give so well,
Un-rehearsed, yet superbly faultless.
Saying "Hi" or "Hello", is your greatest achievement.
Waving "good-bye" to often, your saddest trait.

PROTECTION
Hello's encounter a way toward many goodbyes,
Like needs leading to wants—how much safer to want.
People don't expect as much from you then.

M E

Most likely some of each, a philosopher, fighter,
villain, adventurer, and a "Dreamer".
Being a self-made product from the existence of an
environment that had no permanency, I never became
what one wanted, hoped or wished for.

Living, surviving daily by doing things without
question, whether it was wise or not, just setting the
stage to later question the wisdom of my actions and
soften discovering, I was really not so wise.
Feeling unwanted and always searching for a
comfortable, peaceful place to grow old and later die.

Looking at the lives of others, who appear boring,
stagnant, stale, and motionless, I have had an
interesting life; which rewarded me, leaving me without
everything I ever wanted, a cure for loneliness.

Many, many, many, idiotic scenes, stupid time, ugly
times, but yet fortunate to have happened in my life. A
person who was injured for lack of security,
Personal ties, family skills, and never taking things for
granted or assumption and never saying "THANK
YOU" enough.

Never fitting into the "status quo", always appearing
indifferent, letting bitterness and heartache be quickly
removed from my mind; and always living that a new
day would displace all of yesterday's unpleasant and
unmanageable occurrences.
Furiously unable to comprehend
Hate from Love
I remain a very misunderstood
M E

EPITAPH

Please don't be sad.
I have suffered for so long within my mind, and from
my body
You will smile and say
"HE'S FREE"
If anything need ever be said of me, let it be only,

"HE WAS A MAN THAT REALLY TRIED
HARD"
For survival
For one love
For a utopia

He found all three . . .
Now that he is
FREE.

NO END

Our love
Was like
The smell
Of Autumn Colors

Falling upon
A turkey's tail.
Our love
Is a tale
That I must
Tell
But
It has no end . . .